ANSWERS
FOR THE SKEPTIC
BY R. SCOTT RICHARDS

THE WORD
FOR TODAY

P.O. Box 8000, Costa Mesa, CA 92628

Answers for the Skeptic
by R. Scott Richards
Published by **The Word for Today**
P.O. Box 8000 Costa Mesa CA 92628
http://www.thewordfortoday.org
ISBN 0-936728- 66-3

© 1996 The Word for Today

TABLE OF CONTENTS

Chapter IV

PREFACE

When Luke wrote the message of the gospel to Theophilus, he declared that his desire was to set forth in order a declaration of those things that are most surely believed among us. Luke desired that Theophilus might know the certainty of those things in which he had been instructed.

We seem to be living in a day of spiritual confusion. Paul wrote to the Ephesians that they not be as children, tossed to and fro with every wind of doctrine by the slight of men and the cunning craftiness whereby they lie in wait to deceive. Because of all the confusion in the church today, and the many winds of doctrine that continue to blow through the body of Christ, we felt that it would be good to have various pastors write booklets that would address the issues and give to you the solid biblical basis of what we believe and why we believe it.

Our purpose is that the spiritual house that you build will be set upon the solid foundation of the eternal Word of God, thus we know that it can withstand the fiercest storms.

Pastor Chuck Smith
Calvary Chapel of Costa Mesa, California

CHAPTER I

THE ULTIMATE POP QUIZ

But of Him you are in Christ Jesus, who became for us wisdom from God.

I Corinthians 1:30

No doubt you've experienced the feeling before.

Perhaps it was the time you walked into class without a care in the world, only to see everyone else doing a last minute panic study session before the big exam that you thought was set for next Tuesday. Maybe it was the time your teacher called you to work out a problem on the chalk board, proving to everyone watching that you and algebra hadn't had the pleasure of meeting just yet. Perhaps it was the time the deeply intellectual look of a deer caught in the headlights came over your face as the toughest final exam question in the history of mankind smiled up at you from a quiz sheet.

Lost. Clueless. In over our heads. We all know what it's like to feel that way in school. But few of us ever expected to be put in the same position because we placed our faith in Jesus. But just like a harsh math teacher (with a frown frozen on her face), the unbelieving world has a tough pop quiz prepared for Christians, with your name and mine written across the top of the page!

As believers in Christ we must face the fact that we will be called on to provide answers to some pretty intimidating questions. And the people asking usually won't take, "Uh, can I get back to you later on that?" for an answer.

"Why in the world do you believe that God exists in the first place?"

"C'mon! Everybody knows the Bible is full of mistakes!"

"Sure, Jesus was a good teacher but you really don't believe He is God, do you?"

In all honesty, few of us look forward to facing these moments in the spotlight. But would it surprise you to learn that God wants every believer to be prepared for this ultimate exam?

Consider some advice from a man who knew a thing or two about being put in the spiritual hot seat, Simon Peter. In his first letter he wrote;

> *But sanctify the Lord God in your hearts, and always be ready to give a defense to everyone who asks you a reason for the hope that is in you, with meekness and fear.*
>
> *I Peter 3:15*

"Sounds like good advice," you might be saying, "but how can I be ready to defend my faith when the going gets tough? When someone asks me hard questions about God all I find myself doing is mumbling, or getting mad!"

If that's how you feel when you are called upon to give a reason for the hope that is within you, God has good news for you. There is a better way of dealing with tough questions than running from conflict or railing at those who may have some problems with faith.

In the next few pages we will discover key biblical principles that can help us not just to survive, but thrive in the spiritual hot seat. The Lord desires to lead us with the discernment, confidence and power necessary to hold our own when we are called to share the reason behind our relationship with God. We'll discover:

WHEN TO ANSWER: How to know the difference between those who have sincere questions and those who simply want to shut us down.

WHAT TO ANSWER: Direct, scriptural and powerful answers for the most commonly raised objections to faith in Jesus.

WHY TO ANSWER: An often forgotten goal in spiritual discussions that can cause our defense of the faith to count for all eternity.

After ministering on college campuses for over fifteen years, I have seen faith in Christ attacked by a wide variety of opponents, ranging from serious minded skeptics to certifiable crazies. It is my conviction that God doesn't want us to be satisfied with a shaky faith that we fear will fail under fire. Let's discover why the Word of God has been called an anvil that has worn out many hammers. Let's allow the Lord to strengthen both our knowledge and confidence in His truth that we might see God's promise in Daniel 12:3 fulfilled in our lives;

> *Those who are wise shall shine*
> *Like the brightness of the firmament,*
> *And those who turn many to righteousness,*
> *Like the stars forever and ever.*

CHAPTER II

WHAT TO ANSWER

*Contend earnestly for the faith which was once
for all delivered to the saints.*

Jude 3

When Paul was sharing the good news of
Jesus in Athens, word of his teaching made its
way to a gathering of deep thinkers that met
regularly to "kick around" the latest new ideas.

Intrigued by the concept of a resurrection
from the dead, they made Paul an offer he could
hardly refuse;

*And they took him and brought him to the
Areopagus, saying, "May we know what this new
doctrine is of which you speak?*
*"For you are bringing some strange things to our
ears. Therefore we want to know what these
things mean."*

Acts 17:19-20

Here's a quick quiz: How would you have felt if you had been standing in Paul's shoes? There before you were the brightest and best minds of the entire known world. All eyes were glued on you with two simple questions behind them - what do you Christians believe and why do you believe it?

Truth be told, most of us would have been scared to death. The most natural thing in the world would be to stuff our hands in our pockets, kick at the dirt and mutter something along the lines of, "Uh...Well...I'd really like to tell you about Jesus...But...Ah...That's not my spiritual gift...That's it! I just don't have the gift of evangelism. Why don't you ask my pastor instead?"

What happens when we give in to this amazingly common temptation? We walk away with the nagging feeling that a great opportunity to be used has fallen by the wayside. Our mind becomes clouded with condemning thoughts like, "Wow...what an on-fire Christian *I* turned out to be!" Instead of being a source of joy and excitement in our lives, the idea of sharing the love of Jesus begins looking more and more like a colossal drag!

And so we carefully structure our lives in such a way that we never have to face that kind of moment again. We either insulate ourselves so that the only people we interact with are 100% pure members of the holy huddle, or camouflage ourselves so that even if the unbelievers around us have questions, they'd never think of asking us in the first place.

Is there a way to break this cycle of defeat and discouragement? The Bible shows us a vivid example of a man who faced the giant called *the fear of sharing* head on and walked away with a knock out. As we see how Paul faced his own high noon show down at a place called the Areopagus, we can learn crucial lessons that can move personal evangelism from the confines of fear to a stronghold of freedom and fruitful service to the Lord.

Step #1
Establish Common Ground

Then Paul stood in the midst of the Areopagus and said,

> *Men of Athens, I perceive that in all things you are very religious; for as I was passing through and considering the objects of your worship, I even found an altar with this inscription:*
> *TO THE UNKNOWN GOD.*
> *Therefore, the One whom you worship without knowing, Him I proclaim to you.*
>
> *Acts 17:22-23*

The first insight into effective evangelism that jumps out at us in Paul's approach is his commitment to establishing common ground with his listeners. He presented his remarks from their frame of reference, not his own. Could you imagine what the response would have been like if Paul had said, "Wow! I'd really like to tell you about Jesus. But before I can, why don't you all take a trip to a place called Tarsus, look up a Rabbi named Gamaliel, sit under his teaching for a year or so until you completely understand the Bible, and <u>then</u> I'll tell you the good news!"

Sounds silly doesn't it? But that approach is not all that different from the way many present Jesus to the world in our day. During my non-Christian days, a number of well meaning believers attempted to convert me. But instead of presenting God's truth in a way that I could understand it, all too often I'd hear things like:

HAST THOU BEEN PROPITIATED BY THE BLOOD OF THE LAMB, YEA, VERILY WITH MUCH WAILING AND GNASHING OF TEETH?!!?

A little overstated? OK, but not by much. Hang out in the church long enough and you'll not only make new friends, but also learn to speak to them in a whole new language called

Christianese. The amazing thing about Christianese is that you can speak it all day long around unbelievers and they'll never be able to crack your secret code!

When we share our faith we need to love those we speak to enough to be understandable from their frame of reference. Never assume that the world understands even the most basic Christian concepts or expressions.

Consider the expression, "Born Again." Most believers understand it to describe the new spiritual life we receive from God when we put our trust in Jesus. But what about the average person in the world? We hear about everything from "born again" businessmen to baseball players. The world defines being "born again" as breaking out of a slump, making a dramatic comeback, even just doing better than you used to do!

What a difference we could make if we simply took the time to explain our terms. "You know, when you come to know God, He changes everything about us. It's just like being given a brand new life!"

Instead of blank stares, we may just see the lights go on for the first time!

Step # 2
Explain God Clearly

Having gone the extra mile to establish common ground with his audience, Paul then laid out the truth about God in a clear and unmistakable way.

God, who made the world and everything in it, since He is Lord of heaven and earth, does not dwell in temples made with hands. Nor is He worshiped with men's hands, as though He needed anything, since He gives to all life, breath, and all things. And He has made from one blood every nation of men to dwell on all the face of the earth, and has determined their preappointed times and the boundaries of their habitation, so that they should seek the Lord, in the hope that they might grope for Him and find Him, though He is not far from each one of us; for in Him we live and move and have our being, as also some of your own poets have said, "For we are also His offspring." Therefore since we are the offspring of God, we ought not to think that the Divine Nature is like gold or silver or stone, something shaped by art and man's devising. Truly, these times of ignorance God overlooked, but now commands all men everywhere to repent, because He has appointed a day on which He will judge the world in righteousness by the Man whom He

has ordained. He has given assurance of this to all
by raising Him from the dead.

Acts 17:24-31

Paul hit the Athenians right where they lived. As intensely religious people, idols and places of worship lined their streets. They had even put up an altar labeled, "To whom it may concern," in case they happened to miss some god along the way. How do we worship God? What is He really like? How can we know Him for sure? These were the questions hot and heavy on the hearts of the people of that day. Paul simply and directly shows that Jesus is the answer to them all.

This is the second key guideline we must follow if we want to be used to share the good news effectively. We need to take the time to discover what the burning spiritual questions are of our day and, like Paul, be able to answer them simply and directly.

So what are the questions people most often have for those of us who know God personally? Having had the opportunity to speak with quite a few non-Christians ranging from the hard core skeptic to the honest seeker of truth, I have found that three basic issues come up over and over again. If we are prepared to give a Bible based answer in each of these areas, we can approach almost any opportunity to share with a great deal of confidence.

Question # 1
Does God Exist?

Although most people would like to believe there is a God, they assume that there is really no hard evidence that He exists. Your friendly neighborhood skeptic will often get his jollies by badgering others with lines like, "God is just a Santa Claus for adults! Prove to me that He exists! I dare you!"

Many people are surprised to learn that the Bible does not contain an elaborate argument designed to prove the existence of God. The reason it doesn't is given to us in the book of Romans;

> *For the wrath of God is revealed from heaven against all ungodliness and unrighteousness of men, who suppress the truth in unrighteousness; Because what may be known of God is manifest in them; for God has shown it unto them.*
>
> *Romans 1:18-19*

The reason God never argues for His existence is because, deep within their hearts, all men know He is real. In fact, God has been so unsubtle about His reality, the only way to avoid it is to make a conscious effort to ignore Him.

How has God made His existence known? The Bible gives us two unavoidable examples.

The Presence of God in Nature

In the Psalms, David observed;

The heavens declare the glory of God; and the firmament shows his handiwork.

Day unto day utters speech, and night unto night reveals knowledge.

There is no speech nor language, where their voice is not heard.

Their line has gone out through all the earth, and their words to the end of the world.

Psalm 19:1-4

The Bible tells us that God has left His fingerprints on the handiwork we call the creation. The order, balance and complexity of the environment around us lead us to the conclusion that such design does not arise from accident, but from an intelligent designer. The fact that life exists at all is nothing short of a miracle. As Princeton biology professor, Dr. Edwin Carlston put it, "The probability of life originating from accident is comparable to the probability of the unabridged dictionary resulting from an explosion in a printing factory."

The Presence of God in Human Nature

But there is a type of evidence of God's existence that hits even closer to home. Again in the Psalms we read,

> *As the deer pants for the water brooks,*
> *So pants my soul for You, O God.*
> *My soul thirsts for God, for the living God.*
> *When shall I come and appear before God?*
>
> Psalm 42:1-2

God has placed within the internal nature of man qualities that can only be adequately explained by the work of a Creator. All people have an undeniable need for a sense of purpose and meaning in their lives. Even the famous French atheist Jean Paul Sarte was forced to admit, "Man is absurd but must act as if he were not." There is also a hunger for unconditional love in all people. If life is just an accident, and love no more than a chemical reaction, why do we long for such impossible things? A far more reasonable and consistent conclusion is that man was made in the image and likeness of a purposeful and loving Creator. As the great French philosopher and scientist Pascal observed, "God has placed within the heart of every person a God-shaped vacuum that only He can fill."

QUESTION # 2
WAS JESUS GOD?

For nearly 2,000 years controversy has swirled around the question of the identity of Jesus. Some try to dismiss Him as a myth. Others say He was a gifted teacher or a miracle working prophet. But the Bible insists that the most overwhelming evidence of God's reality wasn't hot wired in our hearts or written in the stars. The Bible tells us that God forever settled the issue of His existence when He made a personal appearance in our world in the person of Jesus Christ.

The apostle John, an eyewitness of the life, death and resurrection of Jesus summed up his experience in this way;

In the beginning was the Word, and the Word was with God, and the Word was God...And the Word became flesh, and dwelt among us, and we beheld His glory, the glory as of the only begotten of the Father, full of grace and truth.

John 1:1,14

Consider for a moment an eye opening question. If God became a man, what would He be like? Among other things it would be reasonable to expect God to live a perfect, miraculous, and unending life. There has only been one man in history who fit that description to a "T". Jesus Himself drove this point home when one of His disciples made a perfectly logical request;

> *Philip said to Him, "Lord, show us the Father, and it is sufficient for us." Jesus said to him, "Have I been with you so long, and yet you have not known Me, Philip? He who has seen Me has seen the Father."*

> *John 14:8-9*

It has been said that we live on a visited planet. God forever settled the issue of His reality by walking among us as one of us.

QUESTION # 3
IS THE BIBLE THE WORD OF GOD?

Perhaps as you've read this chapter you've been thinking, "Great! The Bible does present some real answers to tough questions. But what if someone says, 'OK. But why should I believe in the Bible?' "

First, we need to understand what the Bible claims itself to be. In II Timothy 3:16-17 we read this unavoidably clear statement of the nature of the Scriptures,

> *All Scripture is given by inspiration of God, and is profitable for doctrine, for reproof, for correction, for instruction in righteousness,*

*that the man of God may be perfect, thoroughly
equipped for every good work.*

The word "inspiration" could be literally translated "God-breathed." The Bible claims to be just as reliable a record of the Word of God as we would have if we had heard God speak the words in person, even feeling the breath of His mouth as He spoke.

Well, it certainly is one thing for the Bible to claim to be divinely inspired, but still another thing to prove it. If we were to receive a true message from God it would not be too much to expect it to pass three tests. Is it historically accurate? Is it consistent with itself, with no contradictions in teaching or fact? Does it give us insight and information that would be impossible to get from any other source but God?

Does the Bible pass these tests? Let's take each of these issues one at a time.

Historical Accuracy

Perhaps the most simple and easily verifiable test the Bible must pass to be taken seriously is historical. How accurately has the Bible borne witness to events that have taken place here in this world? As Jesus Himself put it, "If I have told you earthly things and you do not believe, how will you believe if I tell you heavenly things?" (John 3:12)

Not so long ago the idea that the Bible would have anything useful to tell us about history was considered ridiculous. The assured results of science had demonstrated that written language didn't even exist at the time of Moses. Biblical references to cities such as Sodom and Gomorrah or people like the Hittites were considered only myths and legends.

But then something amazing happened. In 1964, archeologists began to excavate a Middle Eastern ruin named Tel Mardikh. There they found the remains of an ancient city called Ebla. By the mid '70s over 7,000 clay tablets were discovered that showed a highly developed form of writing was in use nearly 1,000 years before Moses. In these records of business transactions are references to Sodom and Gomorrah as actual cities and the Hittites as a dominant world empire.

The case of Ebla is not isolated. In fact, archeologists have now come to the conclusion that no discovery has ever contradicted the Biblical record of human history. Archeology has only confirmed the Bible's trust-worthiness.

Doctrinal Consistency

One of the most popular misconceptions that is often thrown out in conversations about the Bible is the subject of contradictions. No doubt, more than once, we've heard skeptics confidently declare, "Everybody knows the Bible contradicts itself!"

The Bible however, has a different view. In the Psalms David declared, "The words of the Lord are pure words, like silver tried in a furnace of earth, purified seven times" (Psalm 12:6).

To be sure, there are some difficult passages in the Bible that require us to dig for their true meaning. But when even the most famous alleged contradictions of the Bible are seen in context, with an understanding of the culture and language of the day, in the vast majority of cases the problems are easily resolved.

Consider a pair of problem passages that are often presented as proof positive that the Bible can't quite get its story straight. In the Sermon on the Mount, Jesus quoted Exodus 21:23-25 as He said, "You have heard that it was said, 'An eye for an eye and a tooth for a tooth.' But I tell you not to resist an evil person. But whoever slaps you on your right cheek, turn the other to him also" (Matthew 5:38-39).

Skeptics go crazy over this verse. "Which do we do? Get even or turn the other cheek? The Bible clearly contradicts itself!"

Does it? An examination of Exodus 21 tells us that God was laying down the civil laws to govern the nation of Israel. In the Sermon on the Mount, Jesus was directing His remarks to the lives of individual people. The fact of the matter is there are certain rights and privileges that are appropriate for a civil government that aren't appropriate for the average person. If someone robbed your house, for the authorities to track down, arrest, try and toss the criminal in jail is considered justice. For you or me to hunt down the burglar, tie him up and imprison him in the basement for 5 years would be considered kidnapping. From God's point of view, civil justice was to be swift, sure and the punishment was to fit the crime. In personal dealings, God's people were to be characterized by mercy and patience, not by an instant desire for revenge.

When we examine the Scriptures fairly, instead of contradictions we find concrete answers.

Supernatural Quality

Some will say, "OK. But just because a book is consistent and historically accurate doesn't mean that God inspired it!" True. But we've saved the Bible's strongest credential for last. In Isaiah 42:8-9, God throws down an interesting challenge;

> *I am the Lord, that is My name; And My glory I will not give to another, nor My praise to graven images. Behold, the former things have come to pass, and new things I declare; before they spring forth I tell you of them.*

Most people with even a vague understanding of the Bible are aware that much of it is devoted to the subject of predictive prophecy. Why is this so crucial? If someone is able to predict the future with 100% accuracy, that tells us two things about them. First, they are not limited by time and can see coming events before they take place. Second, they are also all powerful in order to be able to arrange all possible circumstances in such a way that what they predicted actually comes to pass. To be able to prophesy accurately, 100% of the time, one must either be God, or be directly in touch with God.

The Bible makes this claim, but does it back it up? Consider one of the most awesomely precise predictions we find in the Scriptures;

> *Who has believed our report? And to whom has the arm of the LORD been revealed?*

*For He shall grow up before Him as a tender
plant, and as a root out of a dry ground. He has
no form or comeliness; and when we see Him,
there is no beauty that we should desire Him.*

*He is despised and rejected of men, a Man of
sorrows and acquainted with grief. And we hid,
as it were, our faces from Him; He was despised,
and we did not esteem Him.*

*Surely He has borne our griefs and carried our
sorrows: yet we esteemed Him stricken, smitten
by God, and afflicted.*

*But He was wounded for our transgressions, He
was bruised for our iniquities; the chastisement
for our peace was upon Him, and by His stripes
we are healed.*

*All we like sheep have gone astray; we have
turned, every one, to his own way; and the* LORD
has laid on Him the iniquity of us all.

Isaiah 53:1-6

Although this passage sounds like it came
directly from the mouth of one of Jesus'
disciples, it was written nearly 700 years before
the birth of Christ. This amazing accuracy in
predicting the future is the rule rather than the
exception in the Bible. The supernatural nature
of prophecy confirms that the Bible is in fact the
Word of God.

Step #3
Expect Conflicting Responses

Following the example of Paul in Athens we have seen that he was committed to directly responding to the questions most on the heart of his listeners, in terms they could easily understand. But what kind of results did Paul achieve for his efforts?

And when they heard of the resurrection of the dead, some mocked, while others said, "We will hear you again on this (matter)." So Paul departed from among them. However, some men joined him and believed, among them Dionysius the Aeropagite, a woman named Damaris, and others with them (Acts 17:32-34).

Here we see an example of the three basic responses that accompany a clear presentation of the good news.

A HOSTILE RESPONSE

Some who heard Paul were indignant, even to the point of mocking or trying to make fun of him. Does this mean that Paul's sharing was defective? Not in the slightest. One hard fact of spiritual life we encounter when we share our faith is that some people who are controlled by sin, self or Satan will lash out at anyone who proclaims the truth. Jesus pulled no punches on this subject;

*If the world hates you, you know that it hated Me
before it hated you. If you were of the world, the
world would love its own. Yet because you are
not of the world, but I chose you out of the world,
therefore the world hates you. Remember the
word that I said to you, "A servant is not greater
than his master." If they persecuted Me, they will
also persecute you. If they kept My word, they
will keep yours also.*

John 15:18-20

Sooner or later, if we stand for Jesus, we will
catch our share of grief. It has been said, if we
say the same sort of things Jesus said to the same
sort of people He said them to, we will get what
He got. If classmates, professors, co-workers,
neighbors or even members of your own family
have mocked your faith, know that both Jesus
and Paul encountered the same things. Not bad
company to be included in, is it?

A HO-HUM RESPONSE

Perhaps even more frustrating than out and
out hostility is the "Ho-hum" reaction of the
terminally uncommitted. "Oh, sure, what you
say about God makes sense, but I'm really not
ready to make my mind up on the issue just yet.
Maybe later." Some even believe that getting
right with God is something they will save for
their death bed. "When my number is up, then
I'll get right with the man upstairs."

Over the years I have come to have just one response for this "we will hear you again" crowd: How do you know you will have a death bed? Suppose you are crossing the street one day and the last thing you remember seeing are the letters "GMC" heading straight for your face? There won't be a lot of time then to think about your eternal destiny. The Bible tells us, "In an acceptable time I have heard you, and in the day of salvation I have helped you. Behold, now is the accepted time; behold, now is the day of salvation" (2 Cor. 6:2).

A HEARTFELT RESPONSE

In Acts 17:34 we are told that some men joined Paul and believed. Some have looked at this and, comparing it to the other overwhelming responses recorded in Acts, give Paul a "thumbs down" review for his effort. "There should be tons of fruit when we share, and all Paul had to show for his effort in Athens was a few little grapes!"

I'm sure God didn't look at this with the same perspective. Remember Jesus' words concerning the meaning of effective outreach;

> *What man of you, having an hundred sheep, if he loses one of them, does not leave the ninety-nine in the wilderness, and go after the one which is lost until he finds it?*

And when he has found [it], he lays [it] on his shoulders, rejoicing.

And when he comes home, he calls together [his] friends and neighbors, saying to them, "Rejoice with me, for I have found my sheep which was lost."

I say to you that likewise there will be more joy in heaven over one sinner who repents than over ninety-nine just persons who need no repentance.

Luke 15:4-7

As we share, we need to keep Jesus' point of view in mind. If the Lord uses us to lead thousands to Jesus, that's wonderful. But if we are given the chance to impact even a handful, remember there is no less joy in heaven over that. What God is looking for is not statistical success, but faithfulness and fruitfulness generated by the Holy Spirit. Pursue faithfulness, to share His Word and show His love, and fruitfulness will take care of itself.

CHAPTER III

WHEN TO ANSWER

Do you look at things according to the outward appearance?

II Corinthians 10:7

There are few experiences we go through in life that are a bigger pain than being caught in the act. I discovered this the hard way as an eight year old. One Friday afternoon, two friends of mine came up with a sure fire way to spice up the weekend. "Let's all sneak out at 3 in the morning and meet down at Luke's house!"

Out on the streets at 3 A.M.? It was irresponsible. It was risky. It was poorly thought out. From an 8 year old perspective it sounded perfect! It didn't take much to get all three of us to commit ourselves to this adventure of a lifetime. Besides, it was a fool proof plan. Who would possibly be awake to catch us at that ridiculous hour?

I carefully planned my escape, even placing my noisy wind-up alarm clock under my pillow so I would be the only one who would hear it. Before long, 3 A.M. came and my alarm vibrated me awake. I found myself silently stealing out of the front door and into the welcoming cover of darkness.

As I approached our prearranged meeting point, I encountered the first hitch in our plans. I was the only one standing out in the fog shrouded cul-de-sac. Maybe Luke and Paul overslept. I decided the best thing to do was to sneak into Luke's house and rouse him.

As it turned out, Luke was too groggy (or too chicken!) to get out of bed. This adventure wasn't turning out to be the "fun-fest" I expected. I headed for Luke's front door, ready to call it a night.

Then, that which I greatly feared came to pass. Luke's dad, an airline pilot returning home from some red eye flight, met me as I headed out the front door!

"Uh, what are you doing here, son?"

"Oh, just walking!" I replied, trying my best to look casual.

My only hope was to just keep going and try my best to look like I knew what I was doing. So I headed back up the street the half mile or so to my house.

As I drew near to home I looked up at the telephone lines and prayed for a break down. "Don't call! Please! Please! Please! Don't call!"

As I rounded the corner before my house, I realized I would soon know what my fate would be. If all was dark and calm, I would at least have until morning to figure a way out of this mess. If all the lights were on, I was dead meat.

As the house came into view, my stomach dropped all the way to the pavement. Every light in the house was on, and there on the front porch was the family welcoming committee. My mom looked upset (yet relieved), my big brother had an ear to ear "You're-gonna-get-it-big-time" grin on his face, and my dad simply stared at me with a look that said, "Now I know why guppies eat their young."

I was then escorted into my bedroom. My dad pointed at my bed and uttered the most terrifying words I had ever heard in the English language.

"I will deal with you in the morning."

Following what seemed to be the longest three hours of my life, I paid the price for my poor judgment. Not even my attempt at putting on four pairs of underwear was able to soften the strong right hand of justice.

From my eight year old point of view I couldn't imagine how the pain of getting caught in the act could be any worse. But as the years roll by we discover that the price to be paid for our indiscretions goes up as well. That hard fact of life was driven home with sledge hammer force during an unplanned interruption of an early morning Bible study nearly 2,000 years ago.

> *But Jesus went unto the mount of Olives.*
> *But early in the morning He came again into the temple, and all the people came to Him; and He sat down, and taught them.*
> *Then the scribes and Pharisees brought to Him a woman caught in adultery. And when they had set her in the midst, they say unto Him, "Teacher, this woman was caught in adultery, in the very act.*
> *"Now Moses, in the law, commanded us, that such should be stoned. But what do You say?"*
> *This they said, testing Him, that they might have something of which to accuse Him.*
>
> *John 8:1-6a*

This scripture not only sets the stage for a beautiful picture of God's grace in action, but it can also provide important practical insight into the fine art of defending the faith.

A Surprise Attack

When Jesus left the Mount of Olives and headed for the temple I am sure that He didn't make His way down the road shadow boxing, with the theme from "Rocky" playing in the background. I am also very confident that He didn't begin His time of teaching the people by saying, "Let's get ready to rumble!!" This attack was unexpected, unannounced and clearly out of left field.

One fact of spiritual life we need to accept is that our time on the hot seat usually comes when we least expect it. The day we are prayed up with our copy of "1000 Answers for the Cultist at Your Door" ready, nothing happens. But the day the water heater explodes and the dog eats your two year old's favorite toy and you're already late for an emergency meeting with the boss...well, you know what happens. God's advice?

Preach the word! Be ready in season and out of season. Convince, rebuke, exhort, with all longsuffering.

II Timothy 4:2

A Sophisticated Attack

The second insight we can gain from Jesus' encounter with the scribes and the Pharisees is that the questions God's people have to deal with aren't the product of stupid minds. The issue Jesus faced was no exception. The Bible tells us that Jesus was always "full of grace and truth." In perfect balance He stood for God's Word and God's love for people. As Jesus' opponents shoved this humiliated woman before the crowd, they no doubt thought, "We've got Him now! If He acts in love and tries to save this woman's life we can nail Him for opposing the Scriptures! If He goes along with Moses' Law, we can call Him a hypocrite for talking love but watching this woman die! There's no way out of this one!"

As Christians, we may find ourselves facing equally tough, seemingly no-win issues. This should keep us both in the Word and on our toes. As Peter put it,

> *Be sober, be vigilant; because your adversary the devil walks about like a roaring lion, seeking whom he may devour.*
>
> I Peter 5:8

A Serious Attack

It is also insightful to note the incredible lengths the scribes and Pharisees went to in attempts to discredit Jesus. Notice how they introduced the woman to Jesus and the crowds;

Teacher, this woman was caught in adultery, in the very act.

John 8:4

Does something strike you as a little odd about this whole situation? One outstanding characteristic of adultery is that it is usually committed out of public view. How then did these Pharisees catch this woman "in the act"? Some believe she was the victim of a classic set up. The Pharisees had cooked up their no-win situation for Jesus. Now all they needed was a suitably pathetic adulteress to pull it off. Notice the man involved in this sordid affair is nowhere to be seen. Could he have been commissioned by these religious rulers to supply the sinner for their trap?

Whether this was the case or not, the seriousness of Jesus' accusers is easily seen. They were perfectly willing to sacrifice a human life simply to win an argument! Why were they so serious in their opposition to Jesus? In John chapter 11 they tip their hand in an interesting way;

Then the chief priests and the Pharisees gathered a council and said, "What shall we do? For this Man works many signs.

*"If we let Him alone like this, everyone will
believe in Him, and the Romans will come and
take away both our place and nation."*

John 11:47-48

What bothered these men about Jesus? If He
was right, they were wrong. And if they were
wrong they would lose both their place of
authority and their control over the nation. They
had a vested interest to protect.

Often times we fail to realize that those who
try to grill us for being Christians are feeling a
bit of heat themselves. Running around in the
back of their minds are thoughts like:

"If this person is right about God, I've
wasted 12 years of my life going door-to-door!"

"If Jesus is true, I might have to give up a
life style that I don't think I could quit!"

"If the Bible is God's Word I've been lying to
my classes for the last 20 years!"

"If there is only one way to God, my family
members for generations back aren't with Him!"

Is it any wonder people will sometimes fight
the message of Jesus like their life depended on
it? For those who refuse to trust Him, it does.

The approach, the arguments, even the
anger of the unbeliever aren't anything new.

Jesus faced the same kind of attacks we do today. But more important than recognizing these attacks is knowing how to respond to them. How did Jesus face this tense, emotionally charged situation?

Answering the Unanswerable

But Jesus stooped down, and wrote on the ground with His finger, [as though He did not hear].

So when they continued asking Him, He raised Himself up and said to them, "He who is without sin among you, let him throw a stone at her first."

And again He stooped down and wrote on the ground.

Then those who heard [it], being convicted by [their] conscience, went out one by one, beginning with the oldest, [even] to the last. And Jesus was left alone, and the woman standing in the midst.

When Jesus had raised Himself up and saw no one but the woman, He said to her, "Woman, where are those accusers of yours? Has no one condemned you?"

She said, "No one, Lord." And Jesus said to her, "Neither do I condemn you; go and sin no more."

John 8:6-11

It is clear that the scribes and Pharisees were dumb struck by Jesus' response. What was going on here?

Letters in the Sand

Often times when we get involved in a hotly disputed discussion we make the fatal error of trying to fight fire with fire, or more accurately the flesh with the flesh. We find ourselves "sharing" wonderfully biblical sentiments like, "Oh, yeah? Well, if you weren't such a vile heathen heading for the world's largest weenie roast, you'd know I'm right!" Jesus took a remarkably different approach. Caught in the cross hairs of the Pharisees' hate, He simply stooped down and began writing in the dust.

There has been no shortage of speculation as to just what Jesus wrote. But there really is no need for guess work. Two fascinating Old Testament verses turn the lights on this intriguing question.

> *You have set our iniquities before You, our secret [sins] in the light of Your countenance.*
>
> *Psalm 90:8*

> *O LORD, the hope of Israel, all who forsake You shall be ashamed.*
> *"Those who depart from Me shall be written in the earth, because they have forsaken the LORD, the fountain of living waters."*

It is clear that when Jesus stooped down to write, He was doing far more than just doodling or finding a way to kill some time. The One who searches hearts and minds was down loading a hefty file on the iniquities of this gang of "sin sniffers." And the names weren't changed to protect the not-so-innocent. As the last of these self-righteous reptiles slinked away (no doubt reaching the toe of their sandal over to wipe out this embarrassing evidence), Jesus was then free to extend grace and truth to a woman who was completely open to Jesus' offer of forgiveness.

The Head or the Heart?

So what can we learn from this show down in the temple courts? Oftentimes when we find ourselves defending the faith we aim directly for the head of the opposition. We focus on the intellectual, believing that a more clever argument or a better command of the facts will decide the battle. But when Jesus faced his detractors, He took aim squarely at the heart.

How can we do the same? Our sharing with even the most skeptical unbeliever can become much more fruitful if we commit ourselves to the following three priorities.

The Motive for Asking

Many believers have found themselves "what-about-ed" to death by the unbeliever. "What about all the mistakes in the Bible?" "What about the native in Africa who never heard?" "What about dinosaurs?" After being buried by such a rapid-fire verbal avalanche, we can't even remember all the questions, let alone know where to begin to answer them.

The best response? Before attempting to chase the questioner down any one of a hundred different rabbit trails, get back to basics. Simply pick any one of the objections you can remember and ask, "If I were to answer that question to your satisfaction, would you consider becoming a Christian?" If the answer is yes, either answer the question or promise them that you'll dig for an answer until you find one.

By the way, if you don't know the answer to a question, honesty is always the best policy. Tell the person you will check into the issue and get back to them as quickly as possible. But never try to snow a skeptic. They'll see through you every time. It's hard to claim that we stand for the God of truth while doing a tap dance around a tough issue.

But what if the unbeliever replies, "Me? Consider becoming a Christian? Get serious!!"

Respectfully yet firmly respond, "Then it's clear that your problem with Jesus isn't intellectual. What is it that really keeps you from believing in Him?"

Dangerous? You bet! Some people may boil over when they are challenged on this level. But we might as well deal with the real issue than spend hours chasing a bunch of mental decoys!

The Motive for Anger

Let's face it, most of us would rather enter an angry skunk wrestling contest than deal with a skeptic about to blow their top. But sometimes an emotional outburst can also reveal much about the true condition of a heart and how to reach it.

A friend of mine was a professing atheist. It seemed every time I tried to share he would get angry and an argument would follow. One day, instead of fighting fire with fire, it dawned on me to ask why Christianity got him so hot and bothered. Had there been some Christian in his life that had hurt him in some way? He looked shocked and then told me the sad story of his church experience. His mother was intensely religious and insisted the whole family go to church every Sunday. As a boy, my friend hated church and soon began to get up early to sneak out his window and run away till his family got home. To put an end to it, his mother decided to tie him up in bed every Saturday night. He looked at me and said, "If that's what God is all about, I don't want to have anything to do with Him!" I replied, "If that's what God was all about I wouldn't want anything to do with Him either. But He's not that way. He really loves you."

The fact is that many people have had similarly bad experiences with professing Christians. The key to reaching those who have been burned is not only to uncover the real issue, but to emphasize that while Christians can and do let others down, Jesus never will.

During the TV Evangelist scandals of the '80's I was bombarded by people demanding, "How can you say Christianity is true when (name your favorite religious snake oil salesman) is so corrupt and hypocritical?" I discovered early on that it was a terrific waste of time to try to defend some skunk who used little old ladies' social security checks to buy solid gold shower fixtures. It was much more productive to simply say, "I agree with you. And that's why I don't call you to follow a church or a TV ministry. I challenge you to follow Jesus Christ. If you follow Jesus you'll find that He is no hypocrite."

The Motive for Arrogance

There are other times when we will encounter people who reject God because they believe the position has already been filled —by their own swollen egos.

During the Gulf War, interest in Bible prophecy hit a fever pitch. People were scouring Isaiah and Jeremiah to find out what the Bible said about the fate of Babylon, today's modern Iraq. Chuck Smith and Greg Laurie were invited to be guests on a phone-in talk show to discuss the issue, along with a professor of religion from a major university. As the program progressed, the professor scoffed at the idea that any of the Old Testament books were truly prophetic. He boldly stated that everyone now knows that Isaiah was really written by three different people. Pastor Chuck replied that Jesus quoted from three major sections of Isaiah, and attributed them all to one man, Isaiah the prophet. The professor huffily replied that we now know much more about the Bible than they did in Jesus' day.

Chuck responded, "So you believe that you know more about the Bible than Jesus Christ?"

The professor hemmed and hawed, "Well, yes. I do."

Chuck replied, "I have nothing to say to anyone who thinks he knows more about the Bible than Jesus." And he hung up.

The fact of the matter is there is a time to answer, but also a time to hold our peace. Consider how Jesus dealt with those who desired the approval of men more than God.

And when He was come into the temple, the chief priests and the elders of the people came unto Him as He was teaching, and said, "By what authority doest Thou these things? and who gave Thee this authority?"

> *But Jesus answered and said to them, "I also will ask you one thing, which if you tell Me, I likewise will tell you by what authority I do these things:*
> *"The baptism of John, where was it from? From heaven or from men?" And they reasoned among themselves, saying, "If we say, 'From heaven,' He will say to us, 'Why then did you not believe him?'*
> *"But if we say, 'From men,' we fear the multitude; for all count John as a prophet."*
> *So they answered Jesus, and said, "We do not know." And He said unto them, "Neither will I tell you by what authority I do these things."*
>
> *Matthew 21:24-27*

When to Answer

The first gift God desires to give us to effectively defend the faith is a healthy sense of discernment. It is not enough to have a snappy comeback for every question under the sun or an undefeated record in debate. If we look at sharing God's truth as some kind of battle of wits, we can easily find ourselves winning the battle but losing the war.

How to stay on track? When your moment in the hot seat arrives, pray for the wisdom to see through the smoke screens to the real question being asked. Ask the Lord for the courage to deal with the issues of the heart, not just the head. But most importantly, make it your goal that people see Jesus in you. As we stay close to Jesus, share His Word and demonstrate His love, we will have the right answer for every person.

CHAPTER IV

WHY TO SHARE

For the love of Christ constrains us.

II Corinthians 5:14

For many Christians, sharing the truth about Jesus with the lost and dying world is an awful lot like the way we approach an exercise program. We all know we should be doing it. We make resolutions and commitments and even an occasional stab at making it a part of our daily routine. But like the "Belly Boinger 2000" that looked so good on the infomercial, but now gathers dust in the garage, our involvement in spreading the good news rarely sees the light of day.

What's gone wrong with the harvest? Many books have been written, sermons preached and songs have been sung on the subject. The message? Evangelism is a real drag, but if you loved Jesus enough you'd work up your courage and sense of duty and do it anyway (even if it killed you!).

How do we traditionally respond when we're on the receiving end of these kinds of fiery challenges? First we feel condemned for being such a bunch of spiritual slugs. Then we get scared, wondering if colossal failures like ourselves are even saved in the first place. Finally, the pressure becomes unbearable and we say, "OK! I give up! I'll witness to somebody!!!"

This leads to one of three predictable results:

A. Operation Bible Storm: This approach is devoted to getting evangelism done as quickly as humanly possible. We get a heathen in our sights, swoop in like a B-1 bomber, drop our spiritual bombs and get back to home base as quickly as we can.

B. The Letter Not the Spirit: This strategy allows us to fulfill our obligation to witness without actually sharing a thing. We find a non-believer and have the following conversation:

Christian: You probably don't want to hear about Jesus, right? OK. Sorry for bugging you. See you later!

Non-Christian: Huh?

C. Martyr's Delight: We give ourselves a lifetime guarantee against feeling guilty by not only sharing, but making sure we get persecuted in the process. We open with a warm, bridge-building line like, "HEY YOU! WANNA KNOW WHY PEOPLE LIKE YOU ARE GOING STRAIGHT TO H.E. DOUBLE HOCKEY STICKS?" If all goes according to plan we can wow the local fellowship with the stirring testimony: "How I Got a Black Eye for the Lord."

The tragic thing about these well intentioned, but off the wall responses is how completely unnecessary they are. When we understand the real reason why we should share the good news, half-baked, guilt generated evangelism can become a thing of the past.

The secret of experiencing evangelism as a blessing instead of a burden is found in the words of Jesus in Matthew 11:28-30;

> *Come to Me, all you who labor and are heavy laden, and I will give you rest. Take My yoke upon you and learn from Me, for I am gentle and lowly in heart, and you will find rest for your souls. For My yoke is easy and my burden is light.*

Three eye opening truths contained in this passage can transform defending our faith (as well as any other service to God) from a heavy load to one of the highlight moments of our lives.

The Compulsion Test

In John 10:10, Jesus told us that He came to give us life and that more abundantly. He came that our joy might be full. Sometimes I wonder if that message has filtered down to the pew level in the church. I see so many walking around with all the excitement of a tired basset hound, letting out long sighs and talking about the heavy burdens God has placed on their shoulders.

While that kind of behavior looks spiritual, it is certainly not scriptural. Jesus never said, "Come unto Me all you who are weary and heavy laden, AND I'LL GIVE YOU SOMETHING *REALLY* HEAVY TO CARRY!!"

Contrary to popular opinion, Jesus came to give us rest. This doesn't mean that we'll sit around doing nothing. But those who serve the Lord soon discover that Spirit filled ministry will actually leave us charged up, not punched out. When our service to God is motivated by gratitude and moved by His power there is no greater source of excitement, fulfillment and yes, fun. Even when we are sharing our faith!

If the idea of sharing your faith leaves you feeling weary and heavy laden, take the time to turn back to the Lord, and ask Him to allow you to enter into His rest.

The Closeness Test

Some people see defending the faith as a distraction from the real desire of every Christian, to grow in the grace and knowledge of our Lord Jesus Christ. But from Jesus' point of view, being involved in active service is not a distraction from spiritual growth, but an opportunity to leap forward in the richness of our relationship with Him. Jesus said, "Take My yoke upon you and learn from Me."

One of the most amazing truths about the Christian life is summed up in Luke 6:38;

Give, and it will be given to you: good measure, pressed down, shaken together, and running over will be put into your bosom. For with the same measure that you use, it will be measured back to you.

The fact is, we never learn more in the Christian life than when we are called to teach. We are never blessed more than when we bless others. And ironically enough we never receive more depth of wisdom and insight into our faith than when we give it away to others. Taking the Lord's yoke of reaching out to the lost will free us to learn more from Him than we ever dreamed possible.

The Comfort Test

A critical error many believers make in the realm of defending the faith is looking for some earthly role model in evangelism and assuming that God desires to use us in just the same way. The Bible tells us that we each have gifts that differ from one another. If the Lord had wanted a million Billy Grahams, He would have made a million of them. If the Lord had wanted a million Chuck Smiths, He would have done so. If the Lord had wanted to make a million Greg Lauries or Mike MacIntoshes or Raul Rieses or Jon Coursons or (yikes!) you or me's, He would have.

God delights in doing new and unique works of grace in and through each one of us. When Jesus declared that His yoke was easy, He meant that His kind intention for our lives would suit us perfectly and fulfill us completely. Sometimes we feel like serving the Lord is a chaffing, bruising experience. Perhaps that is because we are trying to wear a yoke that belongs to someone else. Allow the Lord to show you the unique combination of gifts He has given to you. Don't go for canned or cookie cutter approaches to evangelism or any other service to the Lord. You'll discover first hand that Jesus' yoke is easy and His burden really is light.

The Bottom Line

Sometimes we can fall into the trap of "castor oil" Christianity. Like that foul smelling medicine that we forced down because "it was good for us," so we can find ourselves treating our service to God as something to endure rather than enjoy. How can we keep defending the faith from being a burden instead of a blessing? We need to begin to see it not as a "have to," but as a "get to"!

Imagine waking up to a knock on your door one warm summer morning. It's the voice of your trainer yelling, "Get up! You only have two hours before you run for the Olympic gold in the 100 meters!!"

Can you imagine rolling over, putting the pillow over your head and muttering, "Oh, brother...Not again...100 meters is so far to run...Besides there might be someone faster than me out there. I could even pull a muscle or something...But, I guess I'll let a lot of people down if I don't...Oh, alright...I guess I'll get this over with."

Crazy? Having the privilege of running in the Olympic finals is anything but a "have to." And believe it or not, the same applies to another race you and I "get to" have the privilege of running. A fairly successful spiritual runner named Paul had these words to say about this race;

> *For though I am free from all [men], I have made myself a servant to all, that I might win the more; and to the Jews I became as a Jew, that I might win the Jews; to those who are under the law, as under the law, that I might win those who are under the law;*
>
> *to those who are without law, as without law (not being without law toward God, but under the law toward Christ), that I might win those who are without law;*
>
> *to the weak became I as weak, that I might win the weak: I have become all things to all [men], that I might by all means save some.*
>
> *Now this I do for the gospel's sake, that I might be partaker of it with you.*
>
> *Do you not know that those who run in a race all run, but one receives the prize? Run in such a way that you may obtain it.*
>
> *And everyone who competes for the prize is temperate in all things. Now they [do it] to obtain a perishable crown, but we for an imperishable crown.*
>
> *Therefore I run thus: not with uncertainty. Thus I fight: not as one who beats the air.*

> *But I discipline my body and bring [it] into subjection, lest, when I have preached to others, I myself should become disqualified.*
>
> *I Corinthians 9:19-27*

Godspeed as you run your race with joy. See you at the finish line!

Other books available in this series...

Spiritual Warfare
by Brian Brodersen
Pastor Brian Brodersen of Calvary Chapel Vista, California brings biblical balance and practical insight to the subject of spiritual warfare.

Christian Leadership
by Larry Taylor
Pastor Larry Taylor of the Calvary Chapel Bible College in Twin Peaks, California discusses the basics of leadership in the church and challenges us to become leaders that serve.

The Psychologizing of the Faith
by Bob Hoekstra
Pastor Bob Hoekstra of Living in Christ Ministries calls the church to leave the broken cisterns of human wisdom, and to return to the fountain of living water flowing from our wonderful counselor, Jesus Christ.

Practical Christian Living
by Wayne Taylor
Pastor Wayne Taylor of Calvary Fellowship in Seattle, Washington takes us through a study of Romans 12 and 13 showing us what practical Christian living is all about.

Building Godly Character
by Ray Bentley

Pastor Ray Bentley of Maranatha Chapel in San Diego, California takes us through a study in the life of David to show how God builds His character in our individual lives.

Worship and Music Ministry
by Rick Ryan & Dave Newton

Pastor Rick Ryan and Dave Newton of Calvary Chapel Santa Barbara, California give us solid biblical insight into the very important subjects of worship and ministering to the body of Christ through music.

Overcoming Sin & Enjoying God
by Danny Bond

Pastor Danny Bond of Pacific Hills Church in Aliso Viejo, California shows us, through practical principles, that it is possible to live in victory over sin and have constant fellowship with our loving God.

Answers for the Skeptic
by Scott Richards

Pastor Scott Richards of Calvary Fellowship in Tucson, Arizona shows us what to say when our faith is challenged, and how to answer the skeptic in a way that opens hearts to the love and truth of Jesus Christ.

Effective Prayer Life
by Chuck Smith

Pastor Chuck Smith of Calvary Chapel Costa Mesa, California discusses the principles of prayer, the keys to having a dynamic prayer life, and the victorious results of such a life. It will stir in your heart a desire to "pray without ceasing".

Creation by Design
by Mark Eastman, M.D.

Mark Eastman, M.D., of Genesis Outreach in Temecula, California carefully examines and clarifies the evidence for a Creator God, and the reality of His relationship to mankind.

For ordering information, please write to The Word For Today, P.O. Box 8000, Costa Mesa, CA 92628, or call toll free (800) 272-WORD.

How to Become a Christian

First of all you must recognize that you are a sinner. Realize that you have missed the mark. This is true of each of us. We have deliberately crossed the line not once, but many times. The Bible says, "All have sinned and fallen short of the glory of God" (Romans 3:23). This is a hard admission for many to make, but if we are not willing to hear the bad news, we cannot appreciate and respond to the *good news*.

Second, we must realize that Jesus Christ died on the cross for us. Because of sin, God had to take drastic measures to reach us. So He came to this earth and walked here as a man. But Jesus was more than just a good man. He was the God-man—God incarnate—and that is why His death on the cross is so significant.

At the cross, God Himself—in the person of Jesus Christ—took our place and bore our sins. He paid for them and purchased our redemption.

Third, we must repent of our sin. God has commanded men everywhere to repent. Acts 3:19 states, "Repent therefore and be converted, that your sins may be blotted out, so that times of refreshing may come from the presence of the Lord." What does this word *repent* mean? It means to change direction—to hang a U-turn on the road of life. It means to stop living the kind of life we led previously and start living the kind of life outlined in the pages of the Bible. Now we must change and be willing to make a break with the past.

Fourth, we must receive Jesus Christ into our hearts and lives. Being a Christian is having God Himself take residence in our lives. John 1:12 tells us, "But as many as received Him, to them He gave the right to become children of God." We must receive Him. Jesus said, "Behold, I stand at the door and knock. If anyone hears My voice and opens the door, I will come in…" (Revelation 3:20). Each one of us must individually decide to open the door. How do we open it? Through prayer.

If you have never asked Jesus Christ to come into your life, you can do it right now. Here is a suggested prayer you might even pray.

Lord Jesus, I know that I am a sinner and I am sorry for my sin. I turn and repent of my sins right now. Thank You for dying on the cross for me and paying the price for my sin. Please come into my heart and life right now. Fill me with Your Holy Spirit and help me to be Your disciple. Thank You for forgiving me and coming into my life. Thank You that I am now a child of Yours and that I am going to heaven. In Jesus' name, I pray. Amen.

When you pray that prayer God will respond. You have made the right decision–the decision that will impact how you spend eternity. Now you will go to heaven, and in the meantime, find peace and the answers to your spiritual questions.

Taken from: *Life. Any Questions?*
by Greg Laurie, Copyright © 1995. Used by permission.